A Boy Named Mac

WRITTEN BY
Allison Fostveit

ILLUSTRATED BY
Peggy Mink

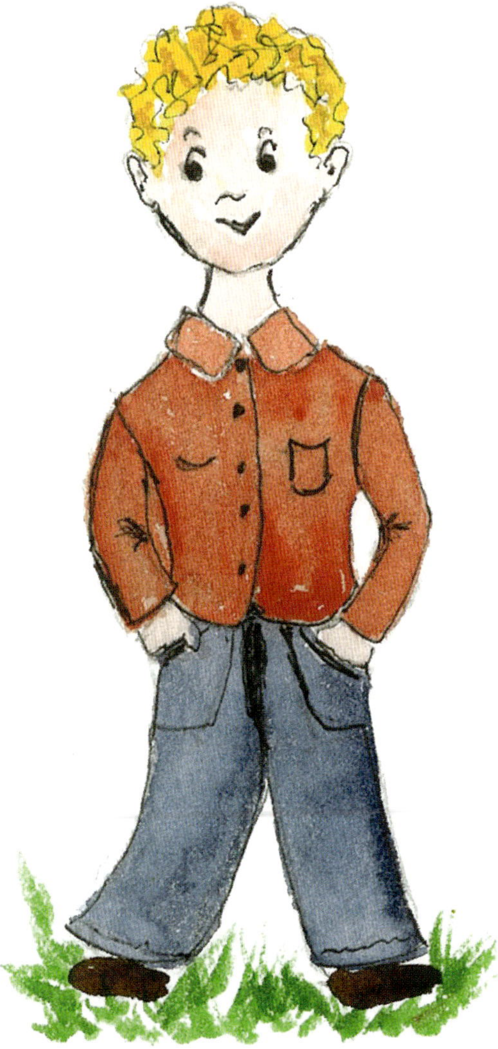

I am a boy, a boy named Mac.

I am a lot like you.

Some things about me are the same,

but there are some differences, too.

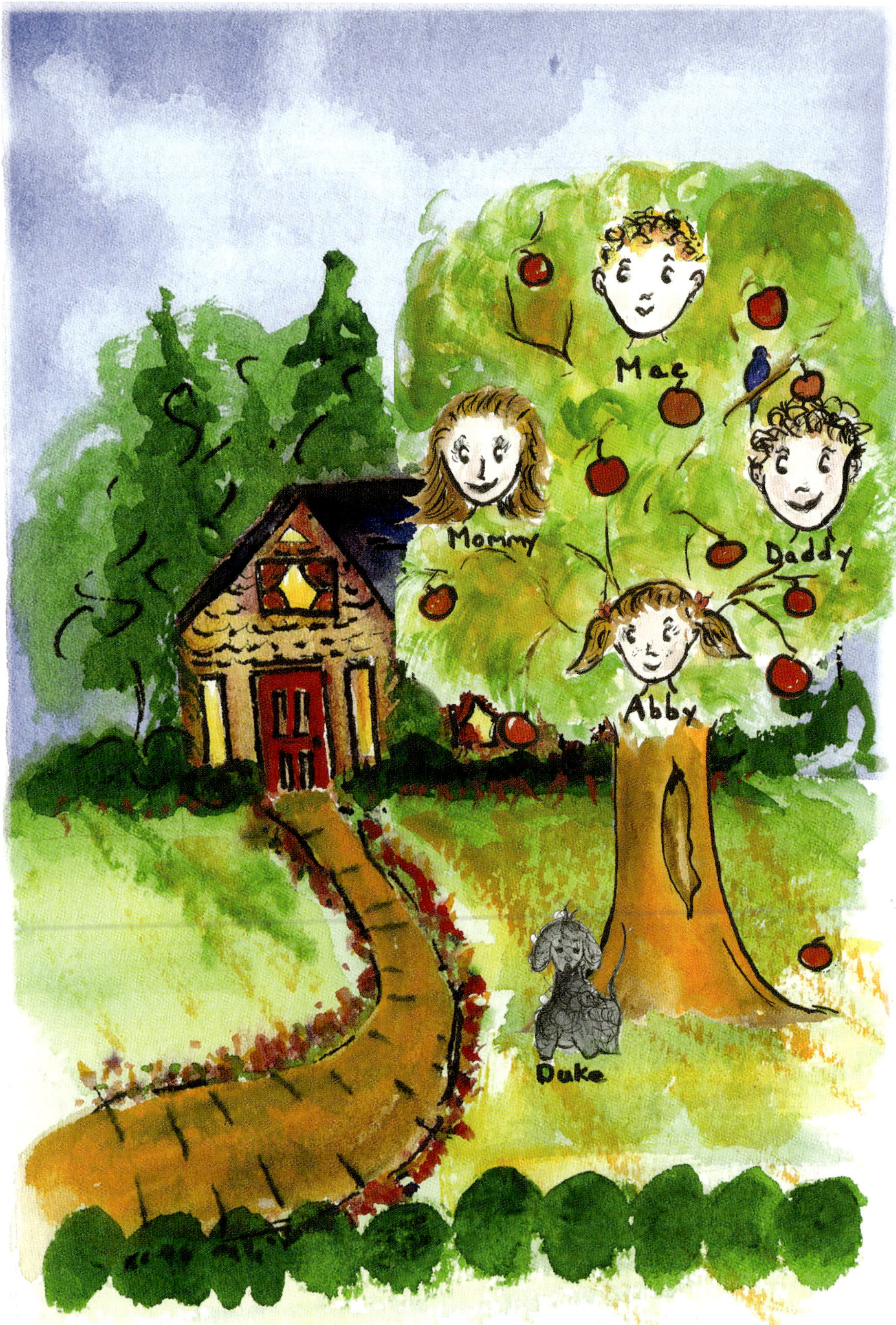
Mac
Mommy
Daddy
Abby
Duke

I live in a house on a cute little street.

This is my family I would like you to meet.

My Mommy, my Daddy, an older sister named Abby.

The family dog, Duke, is big and black.

I throw him a ball and he brings it back.

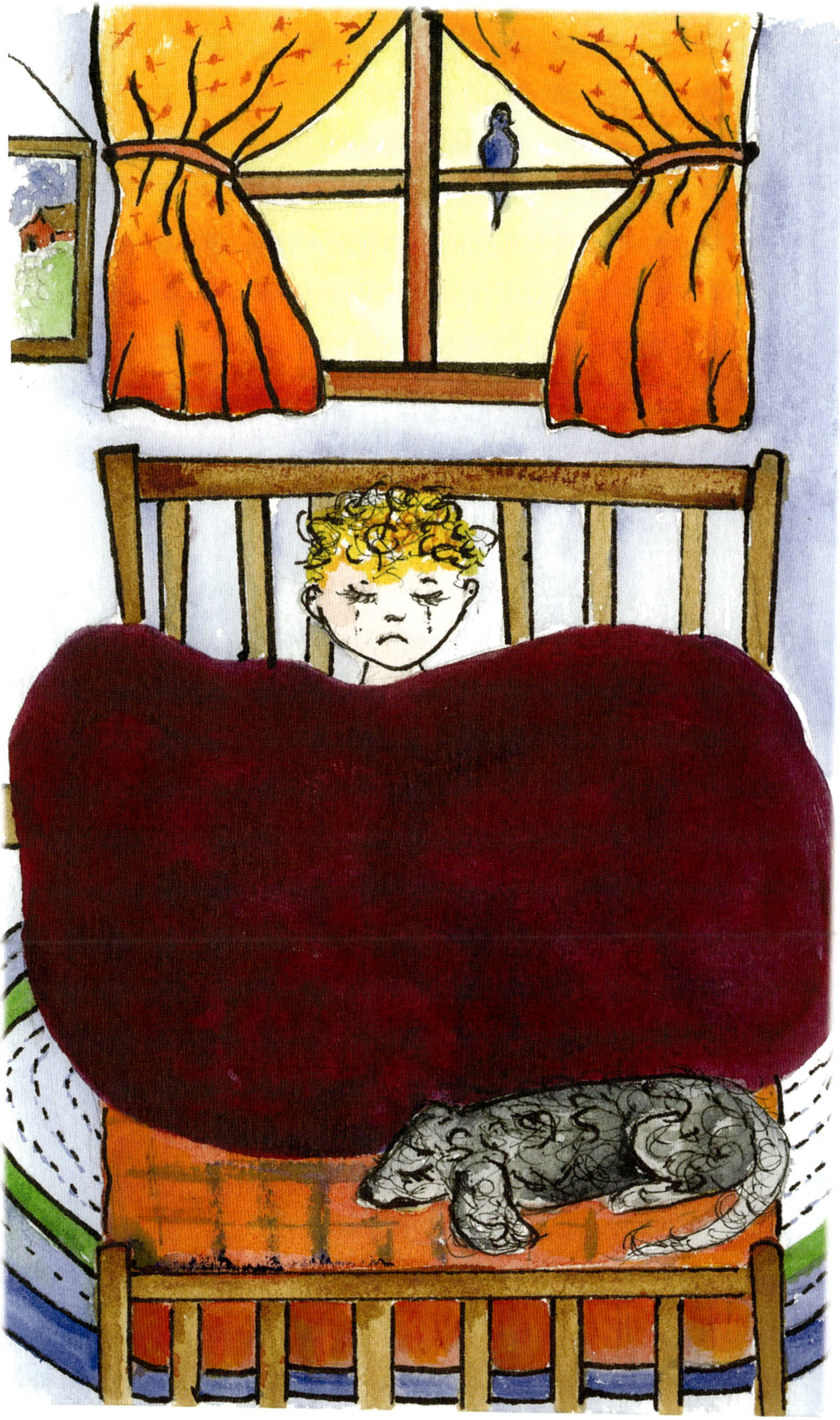

I can have a hard day,
   it can make me feel sad.

I might cry, have a tantrum
   or behave bad.

Using a heavy bean bag
   I can calm myself down.

I will lie underneath it until I
   no longer frown.

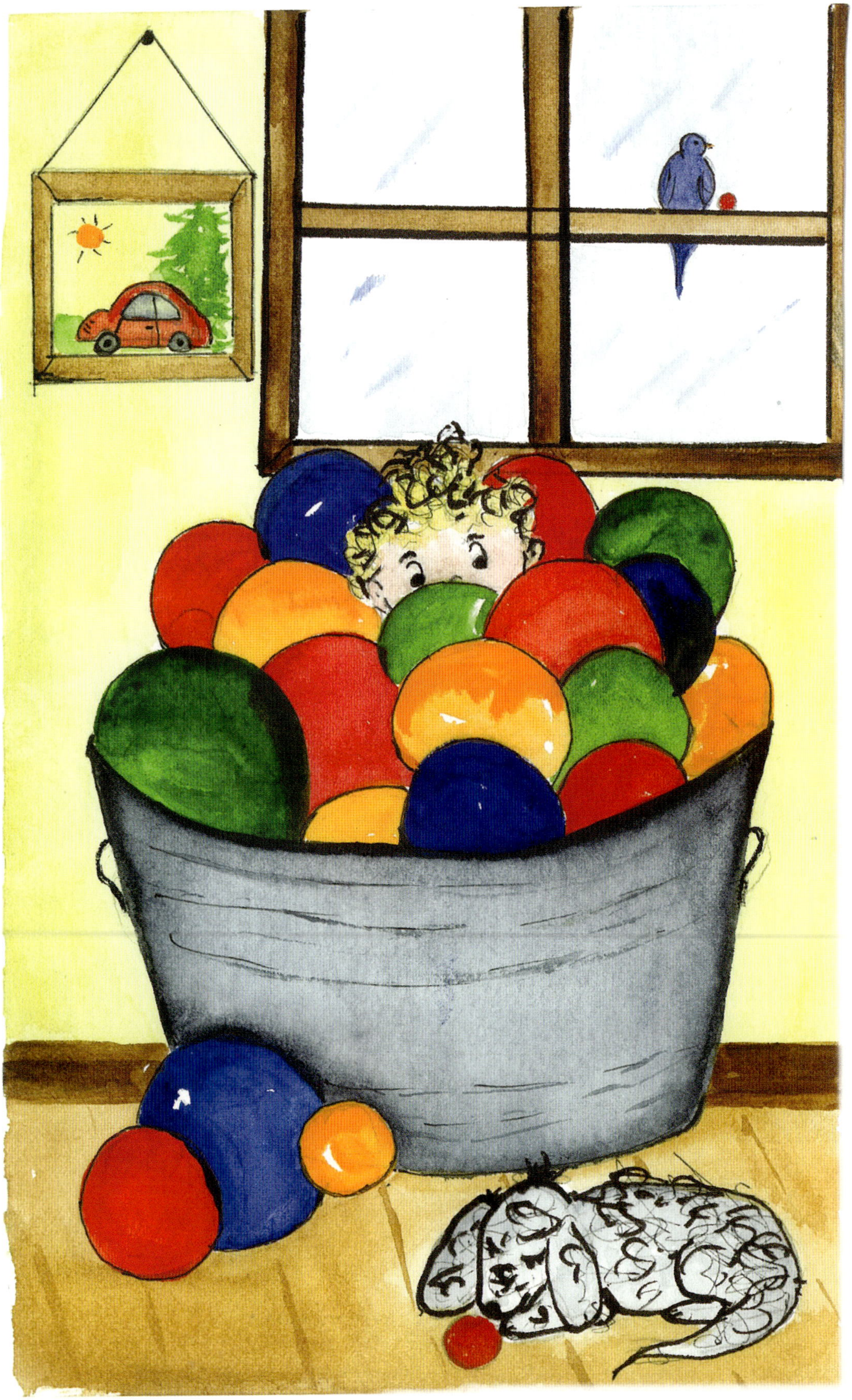

I like to play with toys big and small.

But my favorite thing of all is to play in a tub, a big tub full of balls.

Yellow, green, red and blue,

there are plenty of balls,
 I will share them with you.

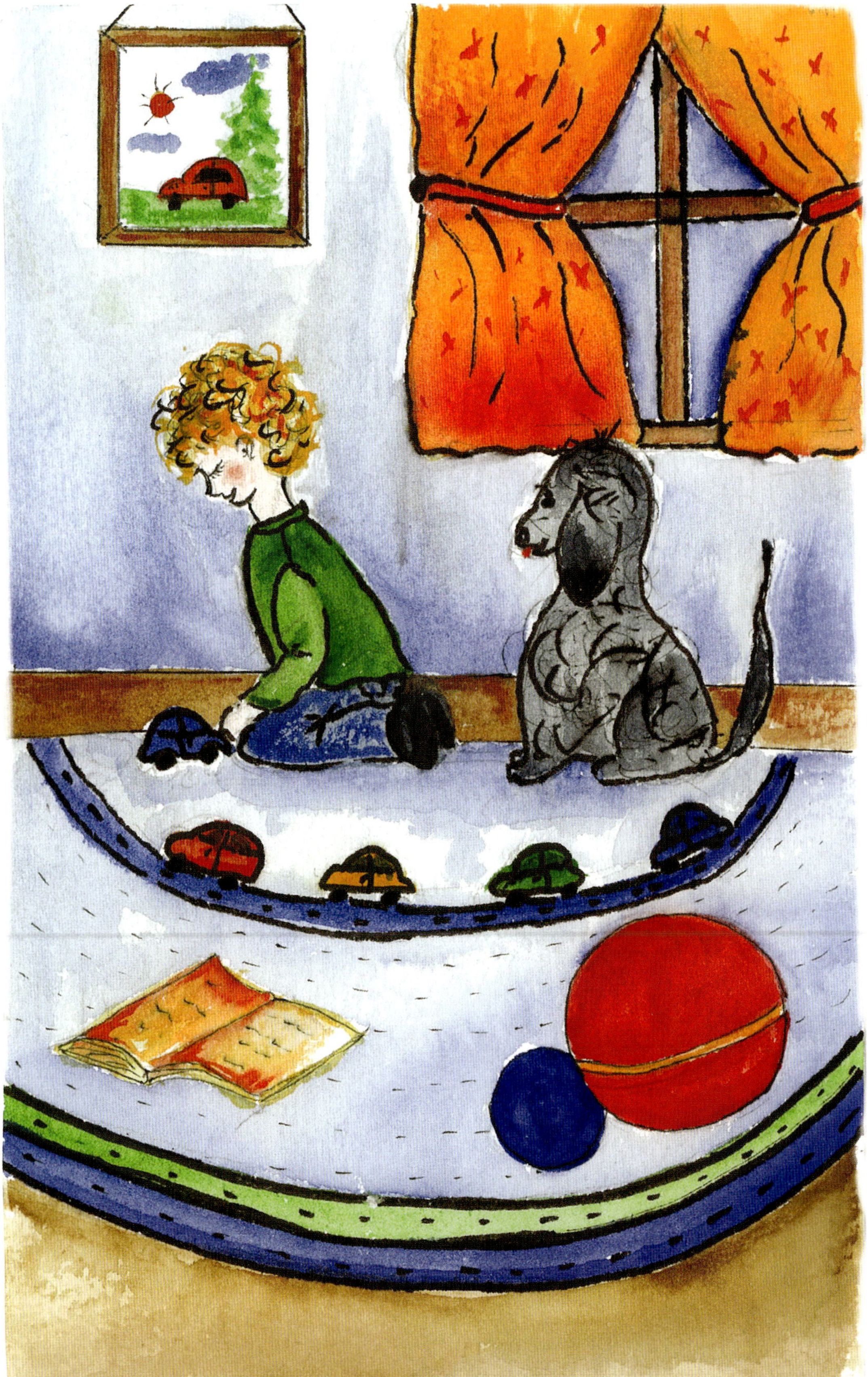

I like to sit by myself on the floor
    and play.

If there are too many people I want
    to go away.

Sometimes it's hard to play
    with other girls and boys.

I am trying to learn to share the books
    and the toys.

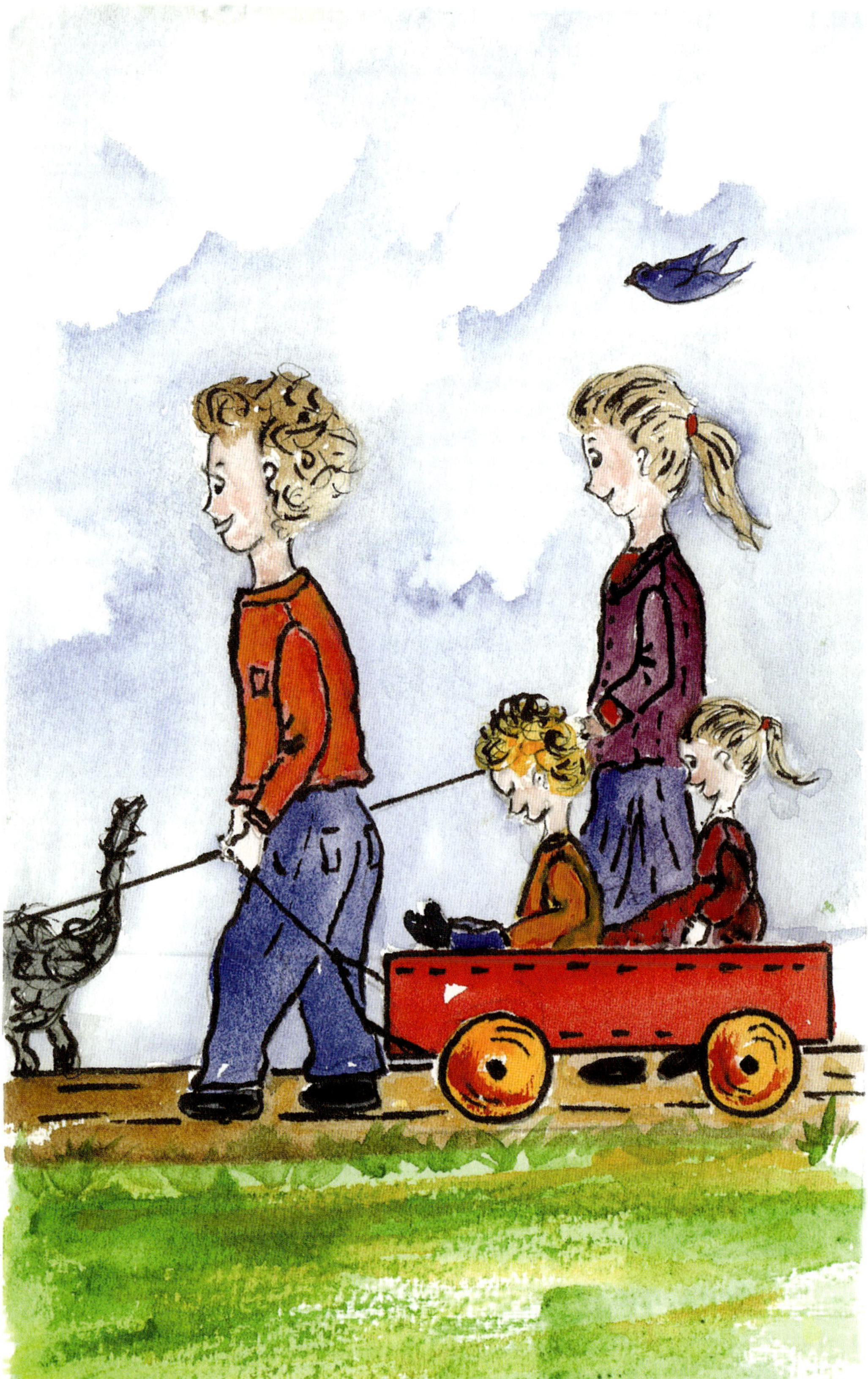

On nice days we might go for a walk

to the playground or just around the block.

Abby and I might ride in a wagon or on a bike.

If the weather is nice we go for as long as we like.

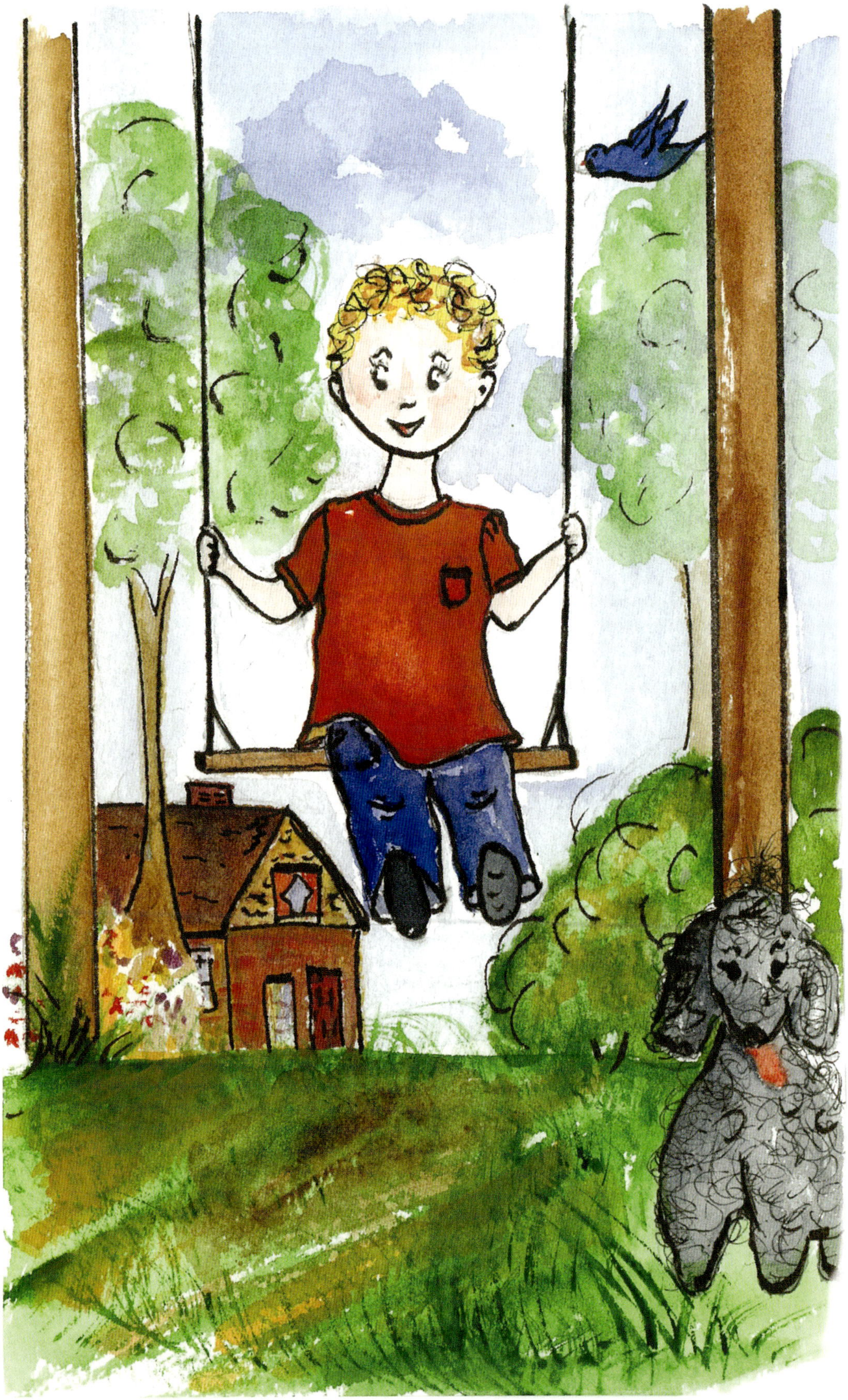

At the playground my favorite thing
   to do is the swing.

It makes me so happy
   that sometimes I sing.

Forward and backward,
   so high it can seem,

when it is time to leave I get mad
   and may scream.

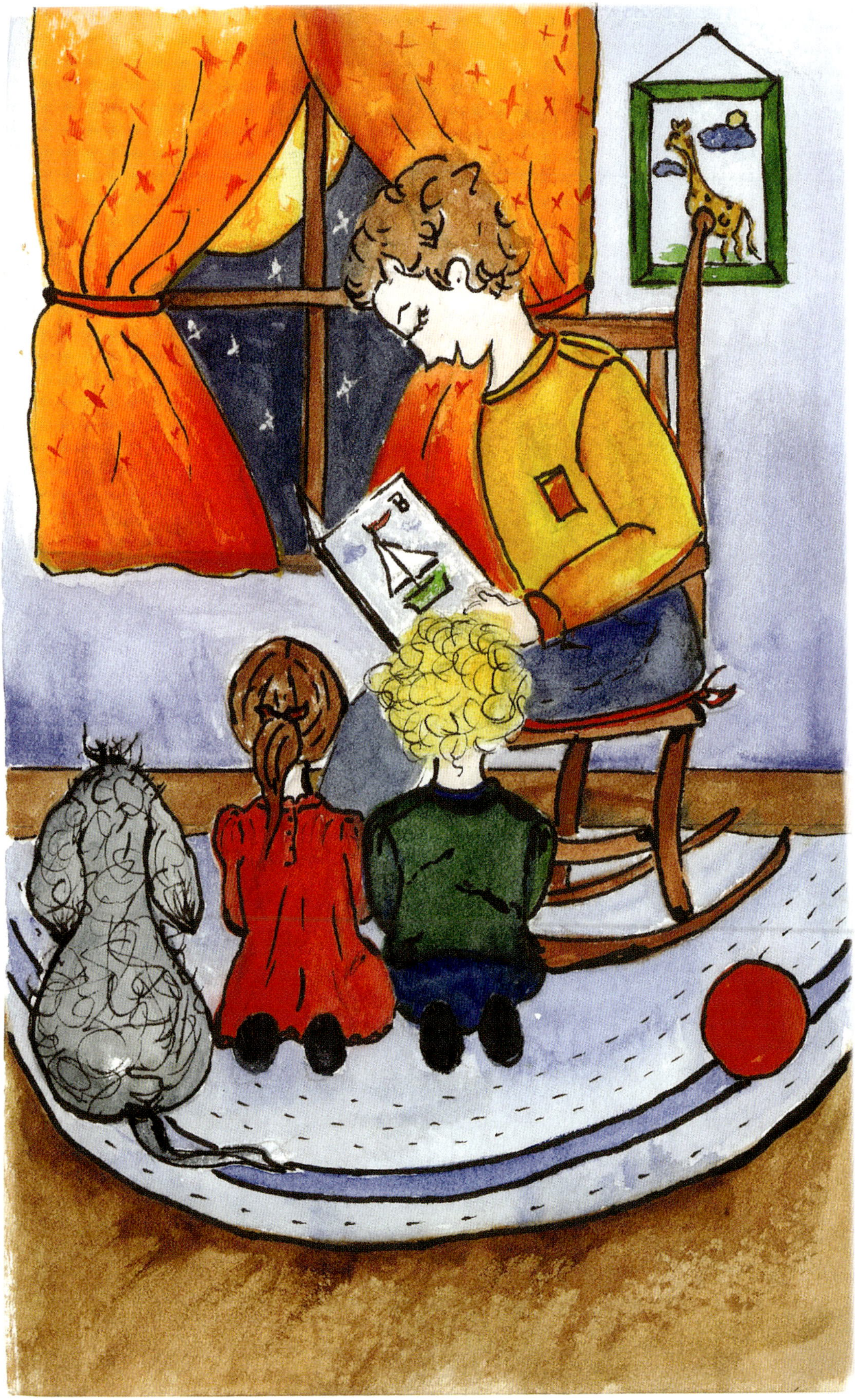

When the day is over and it is night,

Daddy reads to us before we turn out
　　the light.

When the book is done
　　we sing a song.

Daddy sings every night and
　　I like to sing along.

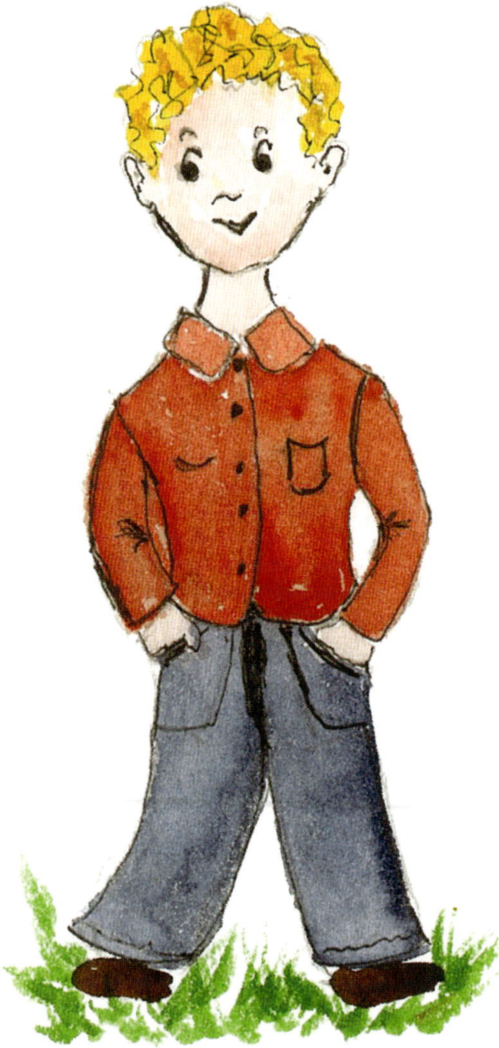

Some things about me are different,

but some are the same.

I have autism and Mac is my name.

I am a boy, a boy named Mac.

I hope to see you again and
 welcome you back.

A Boy Named Mac

www.aboynamedmac.com

Text Copyright © 2009 Allison Fostveit
Illustrations Copyright © 2009 Peggy Mink

All rights reserved. No part of this book may be reproduced by any mechanical, photographic, or electronic process, or in the form of a phonographic recording, nor may it be stored in a retrieval system, transmitted, or otherwise be copied for public or private use without prior written permission from the publisher.

ISBN 978-0-615-34678-6

Printed and Manufactured in China.
10/LP/1